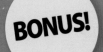

LOOK FOR THE CAMERA in technique videos made just for you!

M000208825

Q-Hook Afghans for the Family

Crocheted with multiple strands of yarn, these afghans are plush and comfy. Once you see how fast they work up, you'll enjoy making them to share.

2

5

8

10

12

16

18

21

24

LEISURE ARTS, INC. • Maumelle, Arkansas

Good Morning

■□□□ **EASY**

Finished Size: 50½" x 70" (128.5 cm x 178 cm)

SHOPPING LIST

Yarn (Bulky Weight)

[3 ounces, 135 yards
(85 grams, 123 meters) per skein]:

☐ 22 skeins

Crochet Hook

☐ Size P/Q (15 mm)

Additional Supplies

☐ Yarn needle

Afghan is worked holding two strands
of yarn together throughout.

GAUGE INFORMATION

Each Center = 13½" (34.25 cm) wide
Each Panel = 15½" (39.25 cm) wide
Rows 1-8 = 8" (20.25 cm)
Gauge Swatch: 13½"w x 8"h
(34.25 cm x 20.25 cm)
Work same as Center for 8 rows: 10 dc,
3 Popcorns, and 6 ch-1 sps.

─── STITCH GUIDE ───

🎥 **POPCORN** (uses one st)
4 Dc in st indicated, drop loop
from hook, insert hook in first dc of
4-dc group, hook dropped loop and
draw through st *(Fig. A)*.

Fig. A

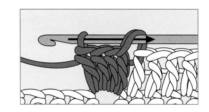

🎥 **V-ST** (uses one st or sp)
(Dc, ch 1, dc) in st or sp indicated.

INSTRUCTIONS
Panel (Make 3)
CENTER

Ch 20.

Row 1: Sc in second ch from hook
and in each ch across: 19 sc.

Row 2 (Right side)**:** Ch 3 (**counts as
first dc, now and throughout**), turn;
dc in next sc and in each sc across.

Note: Loop a short piece of yarn
around any stitch to mark Row 2 as
right side.

Row 3: Ch 1, turn; sc in each dc
across.

Row 4: Ch 3, turn; dc in next 7 sc, ch 1,
skip next sc, work Popcorn in next sc,
ch 1, skip next sc, dc in last 8 sc: 16 dc,
one Popcorn, and 2 ch-1 sps.

Row 5: Ch 1, turn; sc in each st and in each ch-1 sp across: 19 sc.

Row 6: Ch 3, turn; dc in next 5 sc, ch 1, skip next sc, work Popcorn in next sc, ch 1, skip next sc, dc in next sc, ch 1, skip next sc, work Popcorn in next sc, ch 1, skip next sc, dc in last 6 sc: 13 dc, 2 Popcorns, and 4 ch-1 sps.

Row 7: Ch 1, turn; sc in each st and in each ch-1 sp across: 19 sc.

Row 8: Ch 3, turn; dc in next 3 sc, ch 1, skip next sc, work Popcorn in next sc, ch 1, skip next sc, ★ dc in next sc, ch 1, skip next sc, work Popcorn in next sc, ch 1, skip next sc; repeat from ★ once **more**, dc in last 4 sc: 10 dc, 3 Popcorns, and 6 ch-1 sps.

Row 9: Ch 1, turn; sc in each st and in each ch-1 sp across: 19 sc.

Row 10: Ch 3, turn; dc in next 5 sc, ch 1, skip next sc, work Popcorn in next sc, ch 1, skip next sc, dc in next sc, ch 1, skip next sc, work Popcorn in next sc, ch 1, skip next sc, dc in last 6 sc: 13 dc, 2 Popcorns, and 4 ch-1 sps.

Row 11: Ch 1, turn; sc in each st and in each ch-1 sp across: 19 sc.

Row 12: Ch 3, turn; dc in next 7 sc, ch 1, skip next sc, work Popcorn in next sc, ch 1, skip next sc, dc in last 8 sc: 16 dc, one Popcorn, and 2 ch-1 sps.

Row 13: Ch 1, turn; sc in each st and in each ch-1 sp across: 19 sc.

Row 14: Ch 3, turn; dc in next sc and in each sc across.

Row 15: Ch 1, turn; sc in each dc across.

Rows 16-63: Repeat Rows 4-15, 4 times.

Do **not** finish off.

EDGING

Ch 4 (**counts as first dc plus ch 1, now and throughout**), turn; work V-St in first sc, (skip next 2 sc, work V-St in next sc) across to last 3 sc, skip next 2 sc, work (V-St, ch 1, dc) in last sc; † working in end of rows, skip first row, (work V-St in next row, skip next row) across †; working in free loops of beginning ch *(Fig. 1, page 30)*, work (V-St, ch 1, dc) in next ch at base of first sc, (skip next 2 chs, work V-St in next ch) across to last 3 chs, skip next 2 chs, work (V-St, ch 1, dc) in last ch; repeat from † to † once; join with slip st to first dc, finish off.

Assembly

Whipstitch Panels together *(Fig. 3, page 30)*, beginning in center dc of first corner and ending in center dc of next corner.

Border

Rnd 1: With **right** side of short edge facing, join yarn with slip st in center dc of first corner; ch 4, work (dc, ch 1, V-St) in same st, skip next ch-1 sp, work V-St in each ch-1 sp across to within one ch-1 sp of center dc on next corner, skip ch-1 sp, ★ work (V-St, ch 1, V-St) in center dc, skip next ch-1 sp, work V-St in each ch-1 sp across to within one ch-1 sp of center dc on next corner, skip ch-1 sp; repeat from ★ 2 times **more**; join with slip st to first dc.

Rnd 2: (Slip st, ch 4, dc) in next ch-1 sp, work (V-St, ch 1, V-St) in next ch-1 sp, work V-St in each ch-1 sp across to next corner ch-1 sp, ★ work (V-St, ch 1, V-St) in corner ch-1 sp, work V-St in each ch-1 sp across to next corner ch-1 sp; repeat from ★ 2 times **more**; join with slip st to first dc, finish off.

Design by Mary Ann Sipes.

Poinsettias

Shown on page 7.

 INTERMEDIATE

Finished Size: 49" x 63" (124.5 cm x 160 cm)

SHOPPING LIST

Yarn (Medium Weight) 🧶**4**

[7 ounces, 370 yards
(198 grams, 338 meters) per skein]:

☐ Green - 6 skeins
☐ Red - 3 skeins
☐ Gold - 2 skeins

Crochet Hook

☐ Size P/Q (15 mm)

Additional Supplies

☐ Yarn needle

GAUGE INFORMATION

Each Motif = 10½" (26.75 cm)
(straight edge to straight edge)
Gauge Swatch: 3½" (9 cm) diameter
Work same as Motif through Rnd 1:
12 sts.

── STITCH GUIDE ──

🎥 **TREBLE CROCHET**
(abbreviated tr)

YO twice, insert hook in st indicated,
YO and pull up a loop (4 loops on
hook), (YO and draw through 2 loops
on hook) 3 times.

🎥 **CLUSTER** (uses one st)

★ YO, insert hook in st indicated,
YO and pull up a loop, YO and draw
through 2 loops on hook; repeat from
★ once **more**, YO and draw through
all 3 loops on hook.

🎥 **PICOT**

Ch 2, slip st in back ridge of second ch
from hook *(Fig. A)*.

Fig. A

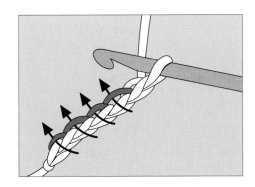

INSTRUCTIONS
Motif (Make 28)

Always push tr to **right** side when
working next sc.

Rnd 1 (Wrong side): With three
strands of Gold, ch 2, (sc, tr) 6 times in
second ch from hook; join with slip st
to first sc, finish off: 12 sts.

Note: Loop a short piece of yarn
around **back** of any stitch on Rnd 1 to
mark **right** side.

Rnd 2: With **right** side facing, 🎥 join
three strands of Red with sc in any tr
(see Joining With Sc, page 29); in next
sc work (slip st, ch 2, Cluster, Picot,
Cluster, ch 2, slip st), ★ sc in next tr,
in next sc work (slip st, ch 2, Cluster,
Picot, Cluster, ch 2, slip st); repeat
from ★ around; join with slip st to first
sc, finish off: 6 petals and 6 sc.

Rnd 3: With **wrong** side facing, join two strands of Green with sc in any sc; ch 3, ★ working in **front** of next petal, sc in next sc, ch 3; repeat from ★ around; working in **front** of last petal, join with slip st to first sc, do **not** finish off: 6 sc and 6 ch-3 sps.

Rnd 4: Ch 3 **(counts as first dc)**, do **not** turn; dc in same st and in next ch-3 sp, working in next petal on Rnd 2, sc in skipped ch on Picot, dc in same sp on Rnd 3 as last dc made, ★ 3 dc in next sc, dc in next ch-3 sp, working in next petal on Rnd 2, sc in skipped ch on Picot, dc in same sp on Rnd 3 as last dc made; repeat from ★ around, dc in same st as first dc; join with slip st to first dc: 36 sts.

Rnd 5: Ch 1, turn; sc in same st and in next 2 dc, 3 sc in next sc, (sc in next 5 dc, 3 sc in next sc) around to last 2 dc, sc in last 2 dc; join with slip st to first sc: 48 sc.

Rnd 6: Ch 1, turn; sc in same st, tr in next sc, sc in next sc, tr in next sc, (sc, tr, sc) in next sc, ★ tr in next sc, (sc in next sc, tr in next sc) 3 times, (sc, tr, sc) in next sc; repeat from ★ around to last 3 sc, tr in next sc, sc in next sc, tr in last sc; join with slip st to first sc, finish off: 60 sts.

Assembly

With two strands of Green and using Placement Diagram as a guide, 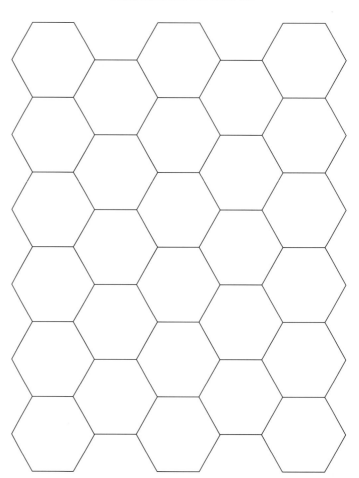 whipstitch Motifs together *(Fig. 3, page 30)* forming 3 vertical strips of 6 Motifs each and 2 vertical strips of 5 Motifs each, beginning in center tr of first corner 3-st group and ending in center tr of next corner 3-st group; then whipstitch strips together in same manner.

Design by Mary Ann Sipes.

PLACEMENT DIAGRAM

Homecoming

◼◼◻◻ **EASY**

Finished Size: 46" x 67" (117 cm x 170 cm)

SHOPPING LIST

Yarn (Medium Weight) **4**
[7 ounces, 370 yards
(198 grams, 338 meters) per skein]:
- ☐ Red - 3 skeins
- ☐ Green - 3 skeins
- ☐ Ecru - 2 skeins

Crochet Hook
- ☐ Size P/Q (15 mm)

Additional Supplies
- ☐ Yarn needle

Afghan is worked holding two strands of yarn together throughout.

GAUGE INFORMATION

In pattern,
 11 sts and 11 rows = 7" (17.75 cm)
Gauge Swatch: 7" (17.75 cm) square
With Red, ch 12.
Work same as Body Rows 1-11: 10 sc
and one ch.

INSTRUCTIONS
Body
With Red, ch 72.

Row 1 (Right side)**:** Sc in second ch from hook and in next 4 chs, ★ ch 1, skip next ch, sc in next 5 chs; repeat from ★ across: 60 sc and 11 ch-1 sps.

Note: Loop a short piece of yarn around any stitch to mark Row 1 as **right** side and bottom edge.

Row 2: Ch 1, turn; sc in first 5 sc, (ch 1, sc in next 5 sc) across.

Row 3: Ch 1, turn; sc in first 5 sc, (ch 1, sc in next 5 sc) across; finish off.

Row 4: With **right** side facing and working in Back Loops Only *(Fig. 2, page 30)*, join Ecru with sc in first sc *(see Joining With Sc, page 29)*; sc in next 4 sc, (ch 1, sc in next 5 sc) across; finish off.

Row 5: With **right** side facing and working in Back Loops Only, join Red with sc in first sc; sc in next 4 sc, (ch 1, sc in next 5 sc) across.

Row 6: Ch 1, turn; working in both loops, sc in first 5 sc, (ch 1, sc in next 5 sc) across.

Row 7: Ch 1, turn; sc in first 5 sc, (ch 1, sc in next 5 sc) across; finish off.

Row 8: With **right** side facing and working in Back Loops Only, join Green with sc in first sc; sc in next 4 sc, (ch 1, sc in next 5 sc) across.

Row 9: Ch 1, turn; working in both loops, sc in first 5 sc, (ch 1, sc in next 5 sc) across.

Row 10: Ch 1, turn; sc in first 5 sc, (ch 1, sc in next 5 sc) across; finish off.

Instructions continued on page 15.

Playroom Wrap

 **EASY**

Finished Size: 41" x 65" (104 cm x 165 cm)

SHOPPING LIST

Yarn (Medium Weight)

[3.5 ounces, 190 yards

(100 grams, 174 meters) per skein]:

- ☐ Black - 8 skeins
- ☐ Red - 2 skeins
- ☐ Blue - 2 skeins
- ☐ Orange - 2 skeins
- ☐ Green - 2 skeins
- ☐ Purple - 1 skein

Crochet Hook

- ☐ Size P/Q (15 mm)

Additional Supplies

- ☐ Yarn needle

Afghan is worked holding two strands of yarn together throughout.

GAUGE INFORMATION

Each Center = 3½" (9 cm) wide

9 sc = 5½" (14 cm)

Gauge Swatch: 3½"w x 9¾"h

(9 cm x 24.75 cm)

With Red, ch 17.

Work same as Center: 16 sc.

INSTRUCTIONS
Strip (Make 9)
CENTER

Make 2 Centers **each** with Red, Blue, Orange, and Green and 1 Center with Purple.

Ch 101.

Row 1: Sc in second ch from hook and in each ch across: 100 sc.

Row 2 (Right side)**:** Ch 3 **(counts as first dc)**, turn; dc in next sc, ★ skip next sc, dc in next 3 sc, working **around** last 3 dc made, dc in skipped sc; repeat from ★ across to last 2 sc, dc in last 2 sc.

Note: Loop a short piece of yarn around first dc to mark Row 2 as **right** side and bottom edge.

Row 3: Ch 1, turn; sc in each dc across; finish off.

EDGING

📹 To work Loop, ch 5, slip st in fifth ch from hook.

With **right** side facing, 📹 join Black with sc in first sc on Row 3 *(see Joining With Sc, page 29)*; work Loop, (sc in next 2 sc, work Loop) across to last sc, sc in last sc; working in end of rows, skip first row, 7 dc in next row, skip last row; working in 📹 free loops of beginning ch *(Fig. 1, page 30)*, sc in ch at base of first sc, work Loop, (sc in next 2 chs, work Loop) across to last ch, sc in last ch; working in end of rows, skip first row, 7 dc in next row, skip last row; join with slip st to first sc, finish off.

Instructions continued on page 15.

Mod Heart

■■□□ **EASY**

Finished Size: 54" x 77½" (137 cm x 197 cm)

SHOPPING LIST

Yarn (Medium Weight)

[4 ounces, 203 yards
(113 grams, 186 meters) per skein]:

☐ 27 skeins

Crochet Hook

☐ Size P/Q (15 mm)

Afghan is worked holding three strands of yarn together throughout.

GAUGE INFORMATION

5 sc and Rows 1-4 = 3¾" (9.5 cm)

Each Panel = 16¾" (42.5 cm) wide

Gauge Swatch: 3¾" (9.5 cm) square

Ch 6.

Work same as Panel Rows 1-4: 5 dc.

Finish off.

—— STITCH GUIDE ——

 TREBLE CROCHET

(abbreviated tr)

YO twice, insert hook in st indicated, YO and pull up a loop (4 loops on hook), (YO and draw through 2 loops on hook) 3 times.

INSTRUCTIONS

Panel (Make 3)

Ch 18.

Row 1: Sc in second ch from hook and in each ch across: 17 sc.

Row 2 (Right side)**:** Ch 3 (**counts as first dc, now and throughout**), turn; dc in next sc and in each sc across.

Note: Loop a short piece of yarn around any stitch to mark Row 2 as **right** side and bottom edge.

Row 3: Ch 1, turn; sc in each dc across.

Row 4: Ch 3, turn; dc in next sc and in each sc across.

Always push tr to **right** side.

Row 5: Ch 1, turn; sc in first dc, (tr in next dc, sc in next dc) across.

Row 6: Ch 3, turn; dc in next tr and in each st across.

Rows 7 and 8: Repeat Rows 3 and 4.

Row 9: Ch 1, turn; sc in first 4 sts, tr in next st, sc in next 7 sts, tr in next st, sc in last 4 sts.

Row 10: Ch 1, turn; sc in first 3 sts, tr in next sc, sc in next tr, tr in next sc, sc in next 5 sts, tr in next sc, sc in next tr, tr in next sc, sc in last 3 sts.

Row 11: Ch 1, turn; sc in first 2 sc, tr in next sc, (sc in next tr, tr in next sc) twice, sc in next 3 sc, tr in next sc, (sc in next tr, tr in next sc) twice, sc in last 2 sc.

Row 12: Repeat Row 10.

Row 13: Repeat Row 9.

Row 14: Ch 3, turn; dc in next sc and in each st across.

Rows 15-20: Repeat Rows 3-6 once, then repeat Rows 3 and 4 once **more**.

Row 21: Ch 1, turn; sc in first 8 dc, tr in next dc, sc in last 8 dc.

Row 22: Ch 1, turn; sc in first 7 sc, tr in next sc, sc in next tr, tr in next sc, sc in last 7 sc.

Row 23: Ch 1, turn; sc in first 6 sc, tr in next sc, sc in next 3 sts, tr in next sc, sc in last 6 sc.

Row 24: Ch 1, turn; sc in first 5 sc, (tr in next sc, sc in next 5 sts) twice.

Row 25: Ch 1, turn; sc in first 4 sc, tr in next sc, sc in next 7 sts, tr in next sc, sc in last 4 sc.

Rows 26 and 27: Ch 1, turn; sc in first 3 sc, tr in next st, (sc in next 4 sts, tr in next st) twice, sc in last 3 sc.

Row 28: Ch 1, turn; sc in first 3 sc, tr in next tr, sc in next 3 sc, tr in next tr, sc in next tr, (tr in next st, sc in next 3 sc) twice.

Row 29: Ch 1, turn; sc in first 4 sts, tr in next sc, sc in next sc, tr in next sc, sc in next 3 sts, tr in next sc, sc in next sc, tr in next sc, sc in last 4 sts.

Row 30: Ch 3, turn; dc in next sc and in each st across.

Rows 31-76: Repeat Rows 3-30 once, then repeat Rows 3-20 once **more**.

Row 77: Ch 1, turn; sc in each dc across; do **not** finish off.

BORDER

Rnd 1: Ch 1, turn; 2 sc in first sc, sc in each sc across to last sc, 3 sc in last sc; working in end of rows, skip first row, 2 sc in each dc row **and** sc in each sc row across to last row, skip last row; working in 🎥 free loops of beginning ch *(Fig. 1, page 30)*, 3 sc in ch at base of first sc, sc in each ch across to last ch, 3 sc in last ch; working in end of rows, skip first row, sc in each sc row **and** 2 sc in each dc row across to last row, skip last row, sc in same st as first sc; join with slip st to first sc: 240 sc.

Rnd 2: Ch 1, turn; (sc, tr) in same st, ★ sc in next sc, (tr in next sc, sc in next sc) across to center sc of next corner 3-sc group, (tr, sc, tr) in center sc; repeat from ★ 2 times **more**, sc in next sc, (tr in next sc, sc in next sc) across, tr in same st as first sc; join with slip st to first sc: 248 sts.

Rnd 3: Ch 1, turn; 3 sc in same st, ★ sc in each st across to center sc of next corner 3-st group, 3 sc in center sc; repeat from ★ 2 times **more**, sc in next tr and in each st across; join with slip st to first sc, finish off: 256 sc.

🎥 Assembly

With **right** side of first Panel facing and bottom edge to right, join yarn with slip st in center sc of first corner 3-sc group; holding **second Panel** with **right** side facing and bottom edge to right, slip st in center sc of corresponding corner 3-sc group, ★ slip st in next sc on **first Panel**, slip st in next sc on **second Panel**; repeat from ★ across to center sc of next 3-sc group on **both** Panels, slip st in center sc on **first Panel**, slip st in center sc on **second Panel**; finish off.

Join remaining Panel in same manner.

Edging

Rnd 1: With **right** side facing and working across short edge of Panels, 📹 join yarn with sc in center sc of first corner 3-sc group *(see Joining With Sc, page 29)*; sc in same st, † sc in each sc and in each joining across to center sc of next corner 3-sc group, 3 sc in center sc, sc in each sc across to center sc of next corner 3-sc group †, 3 sc in center sc; repeat from † to † once, sc in same st as first sc; join with slip st to first sc: 352 sc.

Rnd 2: Ch 4 (**counts as first tr**), turn; sc in same st, ★ † tr in next sc, (sc in next sc, tr in next sc) across to center sc of next corner 3-sc group †, (sc, tr, sc) in center sc; repeat from ★ 2 times **more**, then repeat from † to † once, sc in same st as first tr; join with slip st to first tr: 360 sts.

Rnd 3: Ch 1, turn; 2 sc in same st, ★ † sc in next sc and in each st across to center tr of next corner 3-st group †, 3 sc in center tr; repeat from ★ 2 times **more**, then repeat from † to † once, sc in same st as first sc; join with slip st to first sc: 368 sc.

Rnd 4: Ch 1, do **not** turn; 3 sc in same st, ★ sc in each sc across to center sc of next corner 3-sc group, 3 sc in center sc; repeat from ★ 2 times **more**, sc in each sc across; join with slip st to first sc, finish off.

Design by Mary Ann Sipes.

Homecoming

Instructions continued from page 8.

Row 11: With **right** side facing and working in Back Loops Only, join Ecru with sc in first sc; sc in next 4 sc, (ch 1, sc in next 5 sc) across; finish off.

Rows 12-14: Repeat Rows 8-10.

Rows 15-17: Repeat Rows 5-7.

Rows 18-105: Repeat Rows 4-17, 6 times; then repeat Rows 4-7 once **more**.

📹 VERTICAL STRIPES

Keep yarn to **wrong** side of Afghan.

With **right** side facing and Ecru, insert hook in any ch-1 sp on Row 1 and pull up a loop; working vertically, ★ insert hook in next ch-1 sp in row **above**, YO and draw **loosely** through loop on hook; repeat from ★ across to top edge; finish off.

Repeat for remaining 10 Vertical Stripes.

EDGING

With **right** side facing, join Ecru with slip st in any st; ch 1, 📹 sc evenly around working 3 sc in each corner; join with slip st to first sc, finish off.

Design by Mary Ann Sipes.

Playroom Wrap

Instructions continued from page 10.

Assembly

Afghan is assembled by joining Strips in the following color sequence: Red, Blue, Orange, Green, Purple, Green, Orange, Blue, Red.

📹 Join Strips as follows:

With **right** sides facing, working from bottom to top, Strips side-by-side, and bottom edges toward you, insert hook in first Loop at bottom of **first Strip**, pull first Loop at bottom of **second Strip** through Loop on hook, ★ pull next Loop on **first Strip** through Loop on hook, pull next Loop on **second Strip** through Loop on hook; repeat from ★ across; sew last Loop in place to **first Strip**.

Repeat for remaining Strips.

Braid Loops along outside edge of Afghan in same manner and sew in place.

Design by Mary Ann Sipes.

American Spirit

■■□□□ **EASY**

Finished Size: 47" x 62" (119.5 cm x 157.5 cm)

SHOPPING LIST

Yarn (Medium Weight) 🏷 4

[7 ounces, 364 yards
(198 grams, 333 meters) per skein]:

☐ Off-White - 6 skeins

☐ Blue - 3 skeins

☐ Red - 2 skeins

Crochet Hook

☐ Size P/Q (15 mm)

Additional Supplies

☐ Yarn needle

Afghan is worked holding two strands
of yarn together throughout.

GAUGE INFORMATION

Each Strip = 6¾" (17 cm) wide
    2 rows = 3½" (9 cm)
Gauge Swatch: 4½"w x 7"h
    (11.5 cm x 17.75 cm)
Work same as Center through Row 2:
8 dc and one ch-2 sp.

INSTRUCTIONS
Strip A (Make 4)
CENTER

With Off-White, ch 7; place marker in
third ch from hook for st placement.

Foundation Row (Right side)**:** (3 Dc,
ch 2, 3 dc) in fifth ch from hook, ch 3,
skip next ch, slip st in last ch: 6 dc.

Note: Loop a short piece of yarn
around any stitch to mark Foundation
Row as **right** side and bottom edge.

Row 1: Ch 3 (**counts as first dc,
now and throughout**), do **not**
turn; working in free loops of
beginning ch (**Fig. 1, page 30**), skip
next ch, (3 dc, ch 2, 3 dc) in next ch (at
base of 6-dc group), dc in marked ch:
8 dc and one ch-2 sp.

Rows 2-31: Ch 3, **turn**; (3 dc, ch 2,
3 dc) in next ch-2 sp, skip next 3 dc,
dc in last dc.

Finish off.

EDGING

With **right** side facing, join Blue with
slip st in ch-2 sp on Row 31; ch 3,
(2 dc, ch 2, 3 dc) in same sp, † dc in
next 3 dc; working across end of rows,
2 dc in first row, place marker in last
dc made for joining placement, dc in
same row, 3 dc in each row across to
last row, 2 dc in last row, place marker
in last dc made for joining placement,
dc in same row; dc in next 3 dc †,
(3 dc, ch 2, 3 dc) in next ch-2 sp,
repeat from † to † once; join with
slip st to first dc, finish off.

Strip B (Make 3)
CENTER

Work same as Strip A.

EDGING

With Red, work same as Strip A.

Assembly

Strips are assembled in the following order: Strip A, (Strip B, Strip A) 3 times.

With Red, having bottom edges of 2 Strips at same end, and working through **both** loops on **both** pieces,
whipstitch long edge of Strips together *(Fig. 3, page 30)*, beginning in first marked dc and ending in last marked dc.
Join remaining Strips in same manner.

Design by Maggie Weldon.

Romance

 **EASY**

Finished Size: 48½" x 64" (123 cm x 162.5 cm)

SHOPPING LIST

Yarn (Bulky Weight) **5**

[6 ounces, 185 yards
(170 grams, 169 meters) per skein]:

☐ 8 skeins

Crochet Hook

☐ Size P/Q (15 mm)

GAUGE INFORMATION

In pattern, 5 Star Sts = 5½" (14 cm);
  8 rows = 6" (15.25 cm)
Gauge Swatch: 8¾"w x 3¼"h
  (22.25 cm x 8.25 cm)
Ch 16.
Work same as Body, page 20, for
4 rows: 8 Star Sts.
Finish off.

─── STITCH GUIDE ───

🎥 BEGINNING STAR ST

Insert hook in second ch from hook, YO
and pull up a loop, insert hook in next
ch, YO and pull up a loop, (insert hook
in **next** sc, YO and pull up a loop) twice,
insert hook in next ch-1 sp, YO and pull
up a loop *(Fig. A)*, YO and draw through
all 6 loops on hook, ch 1 to close Star St
and form eyelet.

🎥 STAR ST

Insert hook in eyelet of last Star St
made, YO and pull up a loop, insert
hook in 2 loops on left side of same st,
YO and pull up a loop, insert hook in
same sp as last Star St completed, YO
and pull up a loop, (insert hook in **next**
st or sp, YO and pull up a loop) twice
(Fig. B), YO and draw through all 6 loops
on hook, ch 1 to close Star St and form
eyelet.

🎥 ENDING STAR ST

Insert hook in eyelet of last Star St
made, YO and pull up a loop, insert
hook in 2 loops on left side of same st,
YO and pull up a loop, insert hook in
same st as last Star St completed, YO
and pull up a loop *(Fig. C)*, YO and draw
through all 4 loops on hook.

Fig. A

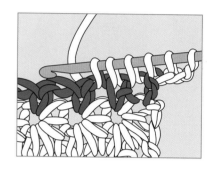

Fig. B

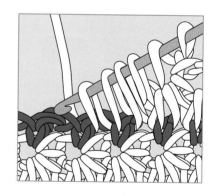

Fig. C

INSTRUCTIONS
Body
Ch 84.

Row 1: Sc in second ch from hook and in next ch, ch 1, ★ skip next ch, sc in next ch, ch 1; repeat from ★ across to last 3 chs, skip next ch, sc in last 2 chs: 43 sc and 40 ch-1 sps.

Row 2 (Right side)**:** Ch 3, turn; work beginning Star St, work Star Sts across, work ending Star St: 42 Star Sts.

Note: Loop a short piece of yarn around any stitch to mark Row 2 as **right** side.

Row 3: Ch 1, turn; sc in first Star St and in eyelet of next Star St, ch 1, (sc in eyelet of next Star St, ch 1) across to last Star St, sc in eyelet of last Star St and in last Star St: 43 sc and 40 ch-1 sps.

Row 4: Ch 3, turn; work beginning Star St, work Star Sts across, work ending Star St: 42 Star Sts.

Repeat Rows 3 and 4 for pattern until Body measures approximately 62" (157.5 cm) from beginning ch, ending by working Row 3; do **not** finish off.

EDGING
Turn; slip st in first sc, (5 hdc in next sc, slip st in next sc) across; † working in end of rows, skip first row, 5 hdc in next row, (slip st in next row, 5 hdc in next row) across to last row, skip last row †; working in ▓ free loops of beginning ch *(Fig. 1, page 30)*, slip st in ch at base of first sc, 5 hdc in next ch, ★ skip next ch, slip st in next ch, skip next ch, 5 hdc in next ch; repeat from ★ across to last ch, slip st in last ch; repeat from † to † once; join with slip st to first slip st, finish off.

Design by Becky Stevens.

Color Pop

Shown on page 23.

◼◻◼◼◻ **INTERMEDIATE**

Finished Size: 50" x 70" (127 cm x 178 cm)

SHOPPING LIST

Yarn (Medium Weight) ④

[5 ounces, 251 yards
(142 grams, 230 meters) per skein]:

☐ Grey - 9 skeins
☐ Rust - 6 skeins
☐ Yellow - 6 skeins

Crochet Hook

☐ Size P/Q (15 mm)

Afghan is worked holding three
strands of yarn together throughout.

GAUGE INFORMATION

In pattern, 5 sc = 4" (10 cm)
    7 rows = 4¼" (10.75 cm)
Gauge Swatch: 8¾"w x 4¼"h
    (22.25 cm x 10.75)
Ch 12.
Work same as Rows 1-7 of Body:
11 sts.
Finish off.

— STITCH GUIDE —

 LONG SINGLE CROCHET
    (abbreviated LSC)
Working **around** previous row(s),
insert hook in st indicated, YO and
pull up a loop even with last st made,
YO and draw through both loops on
hook.

 LONG DOUBLE CROCHET
    (abbreviated LDC)
YO, working **around** previous row(s),
insert hook in st indicated, YO and
pull up a loop even with last st made,
(YO and draw through 2 loops on
hook) twice.

INSTRUCTIONS
Body

With Grey, ch 60.

Row 1 (Right side)**:** Sc in second ch
from hook and in each ch across:
59 sc.

Note: Loop a short piece of yarn
around any stitch to mark Row 1 as
right side.

Row 2: Ch 1, turn; sc in each sc across;
finish off.

Row 3: With **right** side facing,
 join Yellow with sc in first sc *(see
Joining With Sc, page 29)*; sc in next
sc, skip first 3 sc on Row 1, work LDC
in same ch as next sc, sc in next sc
on **previous** row, work LDC in same
st as last LDC made, ★ sc in next sc
on **previous** row, skip next 3 sc on
Row 1 from last LDC made, work LDC
in same ch as next sc, sc in next sc on
previous row, work LDC in same st as
last LDC made; repeat from ★ across
to last 2 sc on **previous** row, sc in last
2 sc.

Row 4: Ch 1, turn; sc in first 3 sts, ★ work LSC in sc one row **below** next sc, sc in next 3 sts on **previous** row; repeat from ★ across; finish off.

Row 5: With **right** side facing, join Grey with sc in first sc; work LDC in sc 2 rows **below** next sc, ★ sc in next 3 sts on **previous** row, work LDC in sc 2 rows **below** next sc; repeat from ★ across to last sc on **previous** row, sc in last sc.

Row 6: Ch 1, turn; sc in each st across; finish off.

Row 7: With **right** side facing, join Rust with sc in first sc; sc in next sc, skip first 3 sc three rows **below**, work LDC in next LSC, sc in next sc on **previous** row, work LDC in same st as last LDC made, ★ sc in next sc on **previous** row, skip next 3 sts three rows **below**, work LDC in next LSC, sc in next sc on **previous** row, work LDC in same st as last LDC made; repeat from ★ across to last 2 sc on **previous** row, sc in last 2 sc.

Row 8: Ch 1, turn; sc in first 3 sts, ★ work LSC in sc one row **below** next sc, sc in next 3 sts on **previous** row; repeat from ★ across; finish off.

Rows 9 and 10: Repeat Rows 5 and 6.

Row 11: With **right** side facing, join Yellow with sc in first sc; sc in next sc, skip first 3 sc three rows **below**, work LDC in next LSC, sc in next sc on **previous** row, work LDC in same st as last LDC made, ★ sc in next sc on **previous** row, skip next 3 sts three rows **below**, work LDC in next LSC, sc in next sc on **previous** row, work LDC in same st as last LDC made; repeat from ★ across to last 2 sc on **previous** row, sc in last 2 sc.

Rows 12-110: Repeat Rows 4-11, 12 times; then repeat Rows 4-6 once **more**.

Edging

Rnd 1: With **right** side facing, join Grey with sc in first sc on Row 110; 2 sc in same st, sc in each st across to last sc, 3 sc in last sc; work 84 sc evenly spaced across end of rows; working in free loops of beginning ch *(Fig. 1, page 30)*, 3 sc in first ch, sc in each ch across to ch at base of last sc, 3 sc in last ch; work 84 sc evenly spaced across end of rows; join with slip st to first sc, finish off: 294 sc.

Rnd 2: With **right** side facing, join Rust with sc in center sc of any corner 3-sc group; 2 sc in same st, sc in each sc around working 3 sc in center sc of each corner 3-sc group; join with slip st to first sc.

Rnd 3: Ch 1, sc in each sc around working 3 sc in center sc of each corner 3-sc group; join with slip st to first sc, finish off.

Design by Mary Ann Sipes.

Sunset Shadows

 EASY

Finished Size: 45" x 60½" (114.5 cm x 153.5 cm)

SHOPPING LIST

Yarn (Medium Weight)

[6 ounces, 315 yards
(170.1 grams, 288 meters) per
skein]:

☐ Black - 4 skeins
☐ Rust - 3 skeins
☐ Peach - 3 skeins
☐ Lt Peach - 3 skeins

Crochet Hook

☐ Size P/Q (15 mm)

Afghan is worked holding two strands
of yarn together throughout.

GAUGE INFORMATION

In pattern, 6 sc = 3½" (9 cm)
    8 rows = 4" (10 cm)
Gauge Swatch: 3½"w x 4"h
    (9 cm x 10 cm)
Ch 7.
Row 1: Sc in second ch from hook
and in each ch across: 6 sc.
Rows 2-8: Ch 1, turn; sc in each sc
across.
Finish off.

TECHNIQUE USED

📹 **CHANGING COLORS**

Work the last sc to within one step of
completion, hook new yarn and draw
through both loops on hook *(Fig. A)*.
Always keep unused color to **wrong**
side. Use separate balls of yarn for
each color change; cut color when no
longer needed.

Fig. A

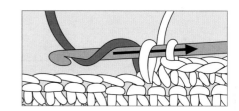

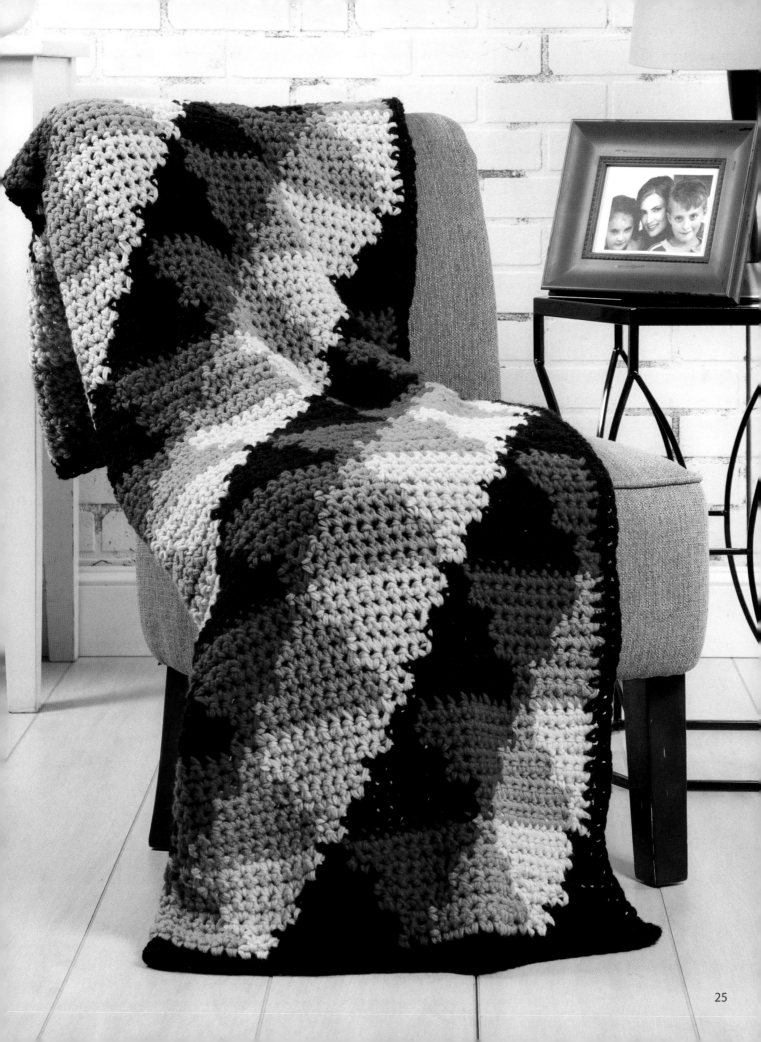

INSTRUCTIONS
Body

With Black, ch 75.

Row 1 (Right side)**:** Sc in second ch from hook and in next 5 chs changing to Lt Peach in last sc made, ★ † sc in next 2 chs changing to Peach in last sc made, sc in next 10 chs changing to Rust in last sc made, sc in next 2 chs changing to Black in last sc made †, sc in next 10 chs changing to Lt Peach in last sc made; repeat from ★ once **more**, then repeat from † to † once, sc in last 6 chs: 74 sc.

Note: Loop a short piece of yarn around any stitch to mark Row 1 as **right** side.

Continue changing colors in same manner throughout.

Row 2: Ch 1, turn; sc in first 6 sc, ★ † with Rust sc in next 2 sc, with Peach sc in next 10 sc, with Lt Peach sc in next 2 sc †, with Black sc in next 10 sc; repeat from ★ once **more**, then repeat from † to † once, with Black sc in last 6 sc.

Row 3: Ch 1, turn; sc in first 6 sc, ★ † with Lt Peach sc in next 2 sc, with Peach sc in next 10 sc, with Rust sc in next 2 sc †, with Black sc in next 10 sc; repeat from ★ once **more**, then repeat from † to † once, with Black sc in last 6 sc.

Row 4: Ch 1, turn; sc in first 4 sc, ★ † with Rust sc in next 6 sc, with Peach sc in next 6 sc, with Lt Peach sc in next 6 sc †, with Black sc in next 6 sc; repeat from ★ once **more**, then repeat from † to † once, with Black sc in last 4 sc.

Row 5: Ch 1, turn; sc in first 4 sc, ★ † with Lt Peach sc in next 6 sc, with Peach sc in next 6 sc, with Rust sc in next 6 sc †, with Black sc in next 6 sc; repeat from ★ once **more**, then repeat from † to † once, with Black sc in last 4 sc.

Row 6: Repeat Row 4.

Row 7: Ch 1, turn; sc in first 2 sc, ★ with Lt Peach sc in next 10 sc, with Peach sc in next 2 sc, with Rust sc in next 10 sc, with Black sc in next 2 sc; repeat from ★ 2 times **more**.

Row 8: Ch 1, turn; sc in first 2 sc, ★ with Rust sc in next 10 sc, with Peach sc in next 2 sc, with Lt Peach sc in next 10 sc, with Black sc in next 2 sc; repeat from ★ 2 times **more**.

Row 9: Repeat Row 7 changing to Lt Peach in last sc.

Row 10: Ch 1, turn; sc in first 2 sc, ★ with Black sc in next 10 sc, with Rust sc in next 2 sc, with Peach sc in next 10 sc, with Lt Peach sc in next 2 sc; repeat from ★ 2 times **more**.

Row 11: Ch 1, turn; sc in first 2 sc, ★ with Peach sc in next 10 sc, with Rust sc in next 2 sc, with Black sc in next 10 sc, with Lt Peach sc in next 2 sc; repeat from ★ 2 times **more**.

Row 12: Repeat Row 10.

Row 13: Ch 1, turn; sc in first 4 sc, ★ † with Peach sc in next 6 sc, with Rust sc in next 6 sc, with Black sc in next 6 sc †, with Lt Peach sc in next 6 sc; repeat from ★ once **more**, then repeat from † to † once, with Lt Peach sc in last 4 sc.

Row 14: Ch 1, turn; sc in first 4 sc, ★ † with Black sc in next 6 sc, with Rust sc in next 6 sc, with Peach sc in next 6 sc †, with Lt Peach sc in next 6 sc; repeat from ★ once **more**, then repeat from † to † once, with Lt Peach sc in last 4 sc.

Row 15: Repeat Row 13.

Row 16: Ch 1, turn; sc in first 6 sc, ★ † with Black sc in next 2 sc, with Rust sc in next 10 sc, with Peach sc in next 2 sc †, with Lt Peach sc in next 10 sc; repeat from ★ once **more**, then repeat from † to † once, with Lt Peach sc in last 6 sc.

Row 17: Ch 1, turn; sc in first 6 sc, ★ † with Peach sc in next 2 sc, with Rust sc in next 10 sc, with Black sc in next 2 sc †, with Lt Peach sc in next 10 sc; repeat from ★ once **more**, then repeat from † to † once, with Lt Peach sc in last 6 sc.

Row 18: Repeat Row 16 changing to Peach in last sc.

Row 19: Ch 1, turn; sc in first 6 sc, ★ † with Rust sc in next 2 sc, with Black sc in next 10 sc, with Lt Peach sc in next 2 sc †, with Peach sc in next 10 sc; repeat from ★ once **more**, then repeat from † to † once, with Peach sc in last 6 sc.

Row 20: Ch 1, turn; sc in first 6 sc, ★ † with Lt Peach sc in next 2 sc, with Black sc in next 10 sc, with Rust sc in next 2 sc †, with Peach sc in next 10 sc; repeat from ★ once **more**, then repeat from † to † once, with Peach sc in last 6 sc.

Row 21: Repeat Row 19.

Row 22: Ch 1, turn; sc in first 4 sc, ★ † with Lt Peach sc in next 6 sc, with Black sc in next 6 sc, with Rust sc in next 6 sc †, with Peach sc in next 6 sc; repeat from ★ once **more**, then repeat from † to † once, with Peach sc in last 4 sc.

Row 23: Ch 1, turn; sc in first 4 sc, ★ † with Rust sc in next 6 sc, with Black sc in next 6 sc, with Lt Peach sc in next 6 sc †, with Peach sc in next 6 sc; repeat from ★ once **more**, then repeat from † to † once, with Peach sc in last 4 sc.

Row 24: Repeat Row 22.

Row 25: Ch 1, turn; sc in first 2 sc, ★ with Rust sc in next 10 sc, with Black sc in next 2 sc, with Lt Peach sc in next 10 sc, with Peach sc in next 2 sc; repeat from ★ 2 times **more**.

Row 26: Ch 1, turn; sc in first 2 sc, ★ with Lt Peach sc in next 10 sc, with Black sc in next 2 sc, with Rust sc in next 10 sc, with Peach sc in next 2 sc; repeat from ★ 2 times **more**.

Row 27: Repeat Row 25 changing to Rust in last sc.

Row 28: Ch 1, turn; sc in first 2 sc, ★ with Peach sc in next 10 sc, with Lt Peach sc in next 2 sc, with Black sc in next 10 sc, with Rust sc in next 2 sc; repeat from ★ 2 times **more**.

Row 29: Ch 1, turn; sc in first 2 sc, ★ with Black sc in next 10 sc, with Lt Peach sc in next 2 sc, with Peach sc in next 10 sc, with Rust sc in next 2 sc; repeat from ★ 2 times **more**.

Row 30: Repeat Row 28.

Row 31: Ch 1, turn; sc in first 4 sc, ★ † with Black sc in next 6 sc, with Lt Peach sc in next 6 sc, with Peach sc in next 6 sc †, with Rust sc in next 6 sc; repeat from ★ once **more**, then repeat from † to † once, with Rust sc in last 4 sc.

Row 32: Ch 1, turn; sc in first 4 sc, ★ † with Peach sc in next 6 sc, with Lt Peach sc in next 6 sc, with Black sc in next 6 sc †, with Rust sc in next 6 sc; repeat from ★ once **more**, then repeat from † to † once, with Rust sc in last 4 sc.

Row 33: Repeat Row 31.

Row 34: Ch 1, turn; sc in first 6 sc, ★ † with Peach sc in next 2 sc, with Lt Peach sc in next 10 sc, with Black sc in next 2 sc †, with Rust sc in next 10 sc; repeat from ★ once **more**, then repeat from † to † once, with Rust sc in last 6 sc.

Row 35: Ch 1, turn; sc in first 6 sc, ★ † with Black sc in next 2 sc, with Lt Peach sc in next 10 sc, with Peach sc in next 2 sc †, with Rust sc in next 10 sc; repeat from ★ once **more**, then repeat from † to † once, with Rust sc in last 6 sc.

Row 36: Repeat Row 34 changing to Black in last sc.

Row 37: Ch 1, turn; sc in first 6 sc, ★ † with Lt Peach sc in next 2 sc, with Peach sc in next 10 sc, with Rust sc in next 2 sc †, with Black sc in next 10 sc; repeat from ★ once **more**, then repeat from † to † once, with Black sc in last 6 sc.

Rows 38-117: Repeat Rows 2-37 twice, then repeat Rows 2-9 once **more**; at end of Row 117 do **not** change colors and do **not** finish off.

EDGING

Rnd 1: With Black ch 1, do **not** turn; sc evenly around entire Afghan working 3 sc in each corner; join with slip st to first sc.

Rnd 2: Ch 1, sc in each sc around working 3 sc in center sc of each corner 3-sc group; join with slip st to first sc, finish off.

Design by Melissa Leapman.

General Instructions

ABBREVIATIONS

ch(s)	chain(s)
cm	centimeters
dc	double crochet(s)
hdc	half double crochet(s)
LDC	Long Double Crochet(s)
LSC	Long Single Crochet(s)
mm	millimeters
Rnd(s)	Round(s)
sc	single crochet(s)
sp(s)	space(s)
st(s)	stitch(es)
tr	treble crochet(s)
YO	yarn over

SYMBOLS & TERMS

★ — work instructions following ★ as many **more** times as indicated in addition to the first time.

† to † — work all instructions from first † to second † **as many** times as specified.

( ) or [ ] — work enclosed instructions **as many** times as specified by the number immediately following **or** work all enclosed instructions in the stitch or space indicated **or** contains explanatory remarks.

colon (:) — the number(s) given after a colon at the end of a row or round denote(s) the number of stitches or spaces you should have on that row or round.

GAUGE

Exact gauge is **essential** for proper size. Before beginning your Afghan, make the sample swatch given in the individual instructions in the yarn and hook specified. After completing the swatch, measure it, counting your stitches and rows or rounds carefully. If your swatch is larger or smaller than specified, keep trying until the correct gauge is obtained.

JOINING WITH SC

When instructed to join with a sc, begin with a slip knot on the hook. Insert the hook in the stitch or space indicated, YO and pull up a loop, YO and draw through both loops on hook.

CROCHET TERMINOLOGY	
UNITED STATES	INTERNATIONAL
slip stitch (slip st)	= single crochet (sc)
single crochet (sc)	= double crochet (dc)
half double crochet (hdc)	= half treble crochet (htr)
double crochet (dc)	= treble crochet (tr)
treble crochet (tr)	= double treble crochet (dtr)
double treble crochet (dtr)	= triple treble crochet (ttr)
triple treble crochet (tr tr)	= quadruple treble crochet (qtr)
skip	= miss

CROCHET HOOKS																
U.S.	B-1	C-2	D-3	E-4	F-5	G-6	7	H-8	I-9	J-10	K-10½	L-11	M/N-13	N/P-15	P/Q	Q	S
Metric - mm	2.25	2.75	3.25	3.5	3.75	4	4.5	5	5.5	6	6.5	8	9	10	15	16	19

FREE LOOPS OF A CHAIN

When instructed to work in free loops of a chain, work in loop indicated by arrow *(Fig. 1)*.

Fig. 1

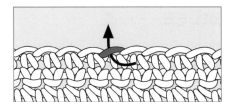

BACK LOOPS ONLY

Work only in loop(s) indicated by arrow *(Fig. 2)*.

Fig. 2

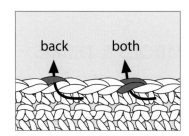

WHIPSTITCH

Place two pieces with **wrong** sides together. Sew through both pieces once to secure the beginning of the seam, leaving an ample yarn end to weave in later. Working through **both** loops of each stitch on **both** pieces, insert the needle from **front** to **back** through first stitch and pull yarn through *(Fig. 3)*, ★ insert the needle from **front** to **back** through next stitch and pull yarn through; repeat from ★ across.

Fig. 3

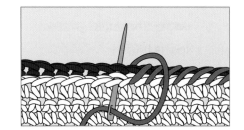

Yarn Weight Symbol & Names	LACE (0)	SUPER FINE (1)	FINE (2)	LIGHT (3)	MEDIUM (4)	BULKY (5)	SUPER BULKY (6)
Type of Yarns in Category	Fingering, 10-count crochet thread	Sock, Fingering Baby	Sport, Baby	DK, Light Worsted	Worsted, Afghan, Aran	Chunky, Craft, Rug	Bulky, Roving
Crochet Gauge* Ranges in Single Crochet to 4" (10 cm)	32-42 double crochets**	21-32 sts	16-20 sts	12-17 sts	11-14 sts	8-11 sts	5-9 sts
Advised Hook Size Range	Steel*** 6,7,8 Regular hook B-1	B-1 to E-4	E-4 to 7	7 to I-9	I-9 to K-10½	K-10½ to M/N-13	M/N-13 and larger

*GUIDELINES ONLY: The chart above reflects the most commonly used gauges and hook sizes for specific yarn categories.

** Lace weight yarns are usually crocheted on larger-size hooks to create lacy openwork patterns. Accordingly, a gauge range is difficult to determine. Always follow the gauge stated in your pattern.

*** Steel crochet hooks are sized differently from regular hooks–the higher the number the smaller the hook, which is the reverse of regular hook sizing.

◼◻◻◻ **BEGINNER**	Projects for first-time crocheters using basic stitches. Minimal shaping.
◼◼◻◻ **EASY**	Projects using yarn with basic stitches, repetitive stitch patterns, simple color changes, and simple shaping and finishing.
◼◼◼◻ **INTERMEDIATE**	Projects using a variety of techniques, such as basic lace patterns or color patterns, mid-level shaping and finishing.
◼◼◼◼ **EXPERIENCED**	Projects with intricate stitch patterns, techniques and dimension, such as non-repeating patterns, multi-color techniques, fine threads, small hooks, detailed shaping and refined finishing.

Yarn Information

The Afghans in this book were made using a variety of yarns. Any brand of yarn in the specified weight may be used. It is best to refer to the yardage/meters when determining how many balls or skeins to purchase. Remember, to arrive at the finished size, it is the GAUGE/TENSION that is important, not the brand of yarn.

For your convenience, listed below are the yarns used to create our photography models.

GOOD MORNING
Lion Brand® Jiffy®
#199 Sky

POINSETTIAS
Red Heart® With Love®
Green - #1621 Evergreen
Red - #1909 Holly Berry
Gold - #1207 Cornsilk

HOMECOMING
Red Heart® With Love®
Red - #1914 Berry Red
Green - #1621 Evergreen
Ecru - #1303 Aran

PLAYROOM WRAP
Red Heart® Classic™
Black - #12 Black
Red - #912 Cherry Red
Blue - #848 Skipper Blue
Orange - #245 Orange
Green - #676 Emerald
Purple - #596 Purple

MOD HEART
Premier® Yarns
Deborah Norville Collection™
Everyday® Soft Worsted
ED100-26 Grenadine

AMERICAN SPIRIT
Red Heart® Super Saver®
Off-White - #313 Aran
Blue - #382 Country
Red - #376 Burgundy

ROMANCE
Lion Brand® Homespun®
#436 Claret

COLOR POP
Lion Brand® Heartland®
Grey - #122 Grand Canyon
Rust - #135 Yosemite
Yellow - #158 Yellowstone

SUNSET SHADOWS
Caron® Simply Soft®
Black - #9727 Black
Rust - #9730 Autumn Red
Peach - #9754 Peach
Lt Peach - #9737 Light County Peach

We have made every effort to ensure that these instructions are accurate and complete. We cannot, however, be responsible for human error, typographical mistakes, or variations in individual work.

Production Team: Instructional Writer/Technical Editor - Linda A. Daley; Editorial Writer - Susan Frantz Wiles; Senior Graphic Artist - Lora Puls; Graphic Artist - Donna Young; Photo Stylist - Sondra Daniels; and Photographer - Justin Bolle.

Afghans made and instructions tested by Janet Akins and Marianna Crowder.